T0084999

# "... AND MY DADDY WILL PLAY THE DRUMS"

## Limericks
### for
### friends
### of
### drummers

## by Warren Benson

With illustrations by the author

Published by
Meredith Music Publications
a division of G.W. Music, Inc.
170 N.E. 33rd St., Ft. Lauderdale, FL 33334


Meredith Music Publications and its stylized double M logo are trademarks
of Meredith Music Publications, a division of G.W. Music, Inc.


Cover design and layout by Warren Benson


No part of this book may be reproduced or transmitted in any form or by any means,
electronic or mechanical, including photocopying, recording or by any informational
storage or retrieval system without permission in writing from the publisher.


International Standard Book Number: 1-57463-067-9


Library of Congress Catalog Card Number: 99-70490


Copyright © 1999 Meredith Music Publications
170 N.E. 33rd St., Ft. Lauderdale, FL 33334
International Copyright Secured.      Printed and bound in U.S.A.      All Rights Reserved.


First Edition
May 1999

for Pat
my dear wife
who knew I was a drummer
and married me anyway


Cameron Warren Benson
my grandson, born on his
dad's birthday, my birthday


Bryce Warren Engelman
son of Robin and Eleanor

Nexus
my students everywhere

With profound thanks to


Gerry Gerard
Jack Ledingham
Arthur Cooper

And especially

Selwyn Alvey


Two Yanks and two Brits

My percussion teachers

From whom I never learned
Anything I'd have to unlearn.

# Contents

# Introduction

During a recent text search I became increasingly frustrated by the scarcity of poetry relating to percussion instruments, church bells and the generic drum excepted. I thought of making a few of my own poems and began to dabble in limericks. Before long, I did find Thoreau, Octavio Paz, Arna Bontemps and Angel Torres (a fifth grader!), completed my new work, "The Drums of Summer," and began a well deserved rest.

A rest, that is, until the itch to continue "limericking" proved compellingly scratchproof.

This collection, therefore, is, finally, at least a present gratification of that itch, exploring historical phenomena, personalities, my friends, bias, opinion and nostalgia, some humorous, some not. No one else should be held responsible . . . guilty . . . or what you will.

Sixty five years a percussionist, I'm still on a roll.

Warren Benson
August 1, 1998
Pittsford, N.Y.

Prelude

These limericks on the drummer's lot
Are as I made them, jewels not;
But rather, blyther,
Authentic neither:
Puns and friends, and all that rot.

## Homemade Accessories

First we'll make some wind chimes from old keys,
A guiro from that veggie grater, please;
    Save heavy auto parts that "pling"—
    The helix of an auto spring,
And don't eschew some Kleenex for a sneeze!
* *Shostakovitch, The Nose, opera (a tutti orchestral sneeze).*

## Celesta

You must sit when you play the celesta.
Stay alert, and don't take a siesta
    Or they'll get someone other,
    Like the Devil's grandmother.
Yet? With her you could have a fiesta!

## The Typewriter*

You don't want to write to Ramona
That you ran with the bulls at Pamplona;
    Just type with the beat
    (And no bull! with the feet),
Whack the "dinger" and play that Corona!
* *by Leroy Anderson*

## Gourmet Gig

Jazz drummers today are just great,
So free and inventive; no freight
    Like that hi-hat lick,
    Going on till you're sick,
Since there's such tasty stuff on their plate.


## Berlioz

I believe he'd had too many ports
When, while scoring his "Grande Messe du Morts,"
    He began to careen,
    Used not two, but sixteen
Roaring kettledrums. Deadly, those snorts.


## Prop?

Lucy's Desi, conga, play it? Riddle.
As much as Henny Youngman played his fiddle!
    But, when Desi had a band
    Before Lucy took command,
Why, then he did what leaders do, they diddle.

for my composer friends in
Wuhan


The bell-tree's the one with that awesome "shing!"
It's a stack of bells on a stick-like thing,
    Like a golden pagoda
    One should save for the Coda
Or use it fulfilling I Ching.


Moroccan Clay Drums


They're colorfully glazed, heads of goat.
Some are large, yet they're easy to tote
    Because there are some
    Just the size of your thumb,
And there's one that got lost in my coat.


Symphony #103

One shouldn't just let them all settle
But attack them at once with a kettle!
    Papa Haydn, quite droll,
    Thus began with a roll
To show London his wit and his mettle.

Kettles Too

They are mounted on horses and camels
And other well trained, sturdy mammals,
    But only a few,
    Like the elephants, who
Are accustomed to timbals,[1] not trammels.[2]

A year and a half in their training[3]
For marching and waiting and raining
    And bystanders shouting
    And drummers "mahouting,"
These pachyderms never complaining.

The horses, "Drum horses," all looming,
Of the Royal Horse Guard, the proud blooming,
    Always lead the parade
    In their silver and braid
And their leather and plumes and their grooming. . .

Their masters must tend to their drums and
                                        their seat,
Staying in tune, keeping lines that are neat,
        If some girls make eyes wander,
        They might find themselves yonder
While the band clatters on up the street.

The cry, "Hi Ho Silver!" is not called for here,
Nor is anything sudden, too quick or severe.
        Then what is our course?
        Why, just ask the horse,
It's the seat of all learning, my dear.
[1] *India: timpani (also, Spain),,* [2] *shackles*
[3] *The Queen's Guard, UK*


Concert by the Lake
Ithaca, 1959


While the maestro hurls program note plums,
A little blonde boy strays from mum's
        Soft restraint toward the flutes;
        Maestro done, blondie toots,
". . . And My Daddy Will Play the Drums!"

Not Your Average Clip, Clop

The "Grand Canyon Suite" works quite well*
At most pop concerts 'cause folks can tell
　　When the donkeys descend
　　To the trail's lower end.
Drink the milk, eat the meat, save the shell.
*Ferde Grofé, coconut shell hoofbeats.


That Certain Age
(Zambia)

Freshly circumsized boys from Lukulu,
In the tribal tradition they grew to,
　　Greet the dawn with a song,
　　Strike two sticks loud and strong,
Come of age, not a tear! What would you do?


Ogane— Great Bell

Sounding one hundred eight rings this year
Will exorcise that many sins, bring cheer.
　　Don't ever give in,
　　Create Ogane's great din!
Then your head, heart and soul will be clear.

That Old Softshoe

"Shhh" is what the sandblocks say.
"Softshoe's" where they make their way:
        "Tea for Two"?
            They'll nicely do.
But "Satin Doll?" <u>No</u> <u>Way</u>!


Flexatone

A metal spatula with arms akimbo,
Shake it side to side— the arms do the limbo.
        You can bend the blade,
            Twang a serenade
As the arms flail away like a raging "bimbo!"*
*sorry, ladies, its neutral!


The Zambezi (stamping sticks)

The thud of the rhythmic pestle and mortar
Is heard upstream to the neighboring border.
        When the women and girls
            Grind their corn, hair in swirls,
Its a heartbeat of very high order.

Playing Down a Storm

A work of art, their finest gong;
The stand for same inspires song!
        In groups, alone,
            Their beauty shone
In whisperings or roaring strong.

They say such gongs will quell a storm,
But how? By loud, or soft, or form?
        In Borneo they know
            The ancient way to go.
We need, I think, their calming norm.


Tire Chains

No, it isn't snowing on the band!
Chains are for effects we need at hand—
        Lowered to the ground
            Or onto timps, the sound
Is creepy, crawly, spooky, understand?

Gourdo

The Cabasa's as round as your head
With no hair, hung with beads in its stead.
    You just twist it and shake it
    And slap it, don't break it.
We'll dance till the dawn just ahead.


Abongo, 1932
[for large percussion ensemble
2 solo dancers and dance group]


And then there's John Becker, a loner,
To the early brave souls, a great donor.
    With percussion en masse
    He gave us some "class"-
Thus earned our Corona Corona!


The World of Percussion

There are so many instruments there,
At least one for each strand of my hair.
    With the former increasing
    And my hair growth now ceasing
There will soon be too many to bare.

Speak to Me

How one may play it is no puzzle.
Keep it 'neath your arm, to nuzzle,
    Squeeze it, make it high or low,
    And tap it with a stick, just so;
A language censors cannot muzzle.


Other Houses— The Bell House

For huge suspended bells with log beams
Horizontal to strike them, it seems
    That the Japanese monks
    Up close hear just "clunks,"
But outside the bell house sound dreams.


Feel Better?

Sick of Dick, that is, Strauss, and so fussy,
Charles V. Stanford just loathed Claude Debussy!
    Thus, his "Ode to Discord"
    Where his "dreadnaught drum" roared!—
Eight feet nine inches wide, <u>very</u> cussy!!

Advert

Why not <u>build</u> a house just for your drum?
In Assam, for slit drums, you'll find some:
    1 rm., riv. vu.
    1 drum, will do.
Have an "open house." Of course, we'll come.


Is That You, Deer?


A percussion ensemble in the sky?
We heard ringing sleighbells up so high
    And thought we missed the list.
    But then someone softly hissed,
"Whoa, Dancer!"
Our Deer Octet is here! We sigh.

This eight of antlered hearties races
Stop to stop in ringing traces,
    None is silent, out of hand
    Till halted, quiet, and, the fat man
        Sings, "Merry Christmas to all, and
            to all Lines and Spaces!"
Then they're off again, ringing, to touch
            all their bases.

## Show-Biz

This composer-conductor from Spain
A haughty, hot-headed migraine,
    Yelled, "Tambour de Provence!"
    Which I nailed!, in response,
Bringing pain to his reign, in the main.


## Washington meets Bobbie?

"They began a low nasal chant". . . he attests,
"Drumming with hands upon their breasts". . .*
    McFerrin was not yet alive
    In eighteen and thirty and five,
When "Tour Prairies" told of Irving's great quests.
*from Oxford English Dictionary, "drum."*


## Manny's Not an Island

"Water, water everywhere, and not a drop to play!"
Bemoaned the beached percussionist whose
                    cruise ship sailed away.
    "My water gong is in Hong Kong,
    My water drum? Salt water's wrong!
God rush the ferry, gentlemen, let nothing you
                    delay!"

Pieces of Reich

That pieces of wood float amazes,
When Steve is in one of his phases.
    His rhythm subliminal
    Is complexly minimal
And tasty, as fine Bordelaise is.


The Desert Fox

There was a young fellow named Rommel—
Spent all his spare time with his trommel.
    He could have gone out
    To play games, jump and shout,
But he'd rather his trommel just
Pummel _____
Pummel _____
Pummel, Pummel, Pummel _____,
Pummel _____
Pummel _____
Pummel, Pummel, Pummel _____.

Gee?

This sweet little lady would sigh, alone;
As she sat, oh so close to her telephone;
    But the phone didn't ring,
    So she did a wise thing—
She went shopping and purchased a xylophone.

Then she called Local 5 about lessons,
And very soon began half hour sessions
    With a drummer unique
    Who, when talking technique,
Would use the most lurid expressions.

They extended her time to an hour,
Moved the place to the lady's sweet bower,
    Closed the telephone book,
    Took the phone off the hook,
As she winked at this Prince in her Tower. . .

But her teacher was so deep in thought
About which of the scales that she ought
    To be studying now
    That she called to him, "Wow!,
Escalation is what we've both sought!"

There's a moral here friends, if you please:
A relationship's all about keys;
    There are some that you play,
    And some you obey,
And some, if you note them, you sieze!


## Jump, Hombre

John Cage and Berio gave a slight nod
To the Mexican Bean in its foot-long dry pod:
    The noise of its rattle
    Could terrify cattle—
Campbell's Beans also thought it quite odd.


## Really BIG DRUM, Japan

Here's a drum one can really get into,
A model "tsuzumi" you begin to
    Carry to some "nth" power:
    It's the Kobe Port Tower,*
The building our hand drum is kin to.
*shaped like the drum, it's 108 m. high.

Traps

Music for whips is no snap,
For good stuff I'd sure tip my cap.
  But most of that gruel
  Isn't fit for a fool,
So you'd better get cracking, old chap!


Off the Wall

Did you know that she played the mbira,
That actress, the great Norma Shira?
  And she still would be on it
  But, while wearing her bonnet,
She played it one day neara mirra!


I'll Drink to That!

There's also a cymbal, a sizzle,
With a riveting sound, like a drizzle
  Of the tiniest spray
  On a fine silver tray,
That you play with a light stick, a swizzle.

It's About Time

It is said that our little Miss Goldilocks
Plays concertos on Korean Temple Blocks.
        Though the music is bland
        She is much in demand
Accompanied by all sorts of ticking clocks.


A Modest Policy

A callow young fellow named Slattery
So enjoyed being part of the battery
        (Since he knew every bit
        That he played was a hit)
That he never, not ever, sought flattery.


Hot Stuff!

In general, if you take it in sum,
You will find we don't use the frame drum.
        We're not like the Inuit,
        Exclusively inu it:
Thrum tum tum, thrum tum tum, thrum tum!

PAREE!

French critics heaped scorn in a pile
On our "bad boy" composer Antheil,
    Since the plane engine's roaring
    (He'd put two in his scoring)
Made his "Ballet Mechanique" a trial.

A bit of an aeroplane freak
Liked <u>only</u> "Ballet Mechanique."
    He thought that a prop
    Was the "raison de trop"
And composer, Antheil, was the peak!


Oh, <u>That</u> Drum

When the tenor of the situation's right,
There's a charm that sums it up that's dynamite:
    Not the piccolo or bass,
    Nor the snare, will suit the case,
Just the one who's name's inherent in that light.

Light "Calvary" Overture

Willie, nervous, well back in the band,
Held his cymbals up, one in each hand,
    As on soared the tune
    Willie played much too soon—
So went Willie's, not Custer's, last stand.

Poor Willie made such an impression
The conductor went into depression,
    The audience clapped,
    One hissed and was slapped,
And poor Willie escaped by secession.


Acqualine

When you lower a gong into water
It will moan like a sad teenaged daughter.
    When it rises, the glow
    Is sufficient to show
She's the buoyant bright thing that you thought'er.

Corona del Arco*

You <u>don't</u> hold this under your chin—
It's long, somewhat flat, fairly thin,
    Yet bowlishly round
    With it's very own sound
And only its bow makes it kin.

Not a drum or a brass or a string,
But a kind of a hardware store thing
    That you bow till it wails
    On its circle of nails
That stick up like the crown on a King.
*nail violin


¡Caramba, Carambanas!

"Cuban Pete" could play the maracas
In rhumbas, clear south to Caracas.
    This nineteen thirties tune
    Made Yankee maidens swoon
But maracas could never afford fine alpacas!

## Stamping Feet

The old Yoruba's poetic request
Expressed the feeling in his aching breast:
   "O, plant me under the dancing ground
   So that I may feel the feet come down.
O, that will make my darkest future blessed."
*I remember this only in paraphrase from various*
*Yorubic sources some 30+ years ago—*
*among them, Ulli Beier, anthropologist.*


## Downsizing

"Paradiddle Joe" was the name of the song
  And a Big Band "hit", but not for long:
    Solo single and double
    And a triple; all trouble
Were the Beatles, quadruple, and Big Bands Be Gone!


## The Duke

But Ellington and Strayhorn thought big,
An opera, in jazz, they did rig:
    "A Drum Is a Woman,"*
    Where this mythical human
Could snare a mate in a beat. You dig?
* *A drum is transformed into Madam Zzaj.*

The Core of Things

Rum jigga Dum jigga Dum zhum Zhum,
Rum jigga Jigga dum Dum Zhum Jum.
    Rigga jigga Jum digga
    Zhigga digga Bum jigga,
Rum jum Jigga digga Jigga zhum Djum!


When the Last Time Zone Strikes Midnight

Better to fail almost any rough test
Than miss the Millennium Drum-In fest.*
    If midnight should sound
    And you're not around,
There is no "next time" for second best!
*1-800-442-DRUM, *even if you are in denial.*


Dance, Anyone?

Rome wouldn't have burned if dear Nero
Had reached in his kit for his guiro
    And gone scratchity scratch,
    Thus forsaking that match,
Flame, and out of tune fiddle, no hero.

for Jack
## The Canadian Recycling Rag*

Take this music, you play it on junk:
It goes Shhh, or goes Whap!, or goes Clunk!
    Steel wool, foam or paper,
    They're all in this caper—
Such voices and sounds from my trunk.
    Let's throw less away,
    Give ideas more play.
All it takes is some time and the spunk
    To re-use-cycle-duce
    As you shake yourself loose
With a Thwang!Blop!Zing!PhuzzStipp!Bam!Thunk!
*for a new work, "The Drums of Summer," whose
second movement calls for six solo percussion plus
fourteen ensemble members playing trash-cum-
instruments, 20 percussion in all.


"Segue!"

In league with old Capulet, Montague
Had his son rhyme his name, saying, "seegyou."
    But that's not the way
    To have Romeo play,
Since Juliet's "segway's" what lovers do.

C. D. 3
Fall, 1957


Welcoming our morning arrival,
The principal spoke of survival
    And his search for the creature
    Who'd encouraged his teacher*
To collect "all those nail kegs" archival.

At thirty he'd imposed a hard ceiling,
"No more!" he'd said, loudly, with feeling.
    The kids added no more,
    Just "bettered" their store
With new ones each day. He was reeling.

They showed us the drums they had made,
And their "stairways" that were for the aid
    Of the short kids and tall.
    There was some height for all
To stand up and play. Escalade. . .

Aluminum cymbals that sizzled,
Fibre-barrel-lid-gongs that drizzled
　　From lamp chains attached.
　　And other sounds they'd matched.
Ensemble! Despite budgets fizzled.

They'd also adopted a name,
"City District School 3?" Not their game!
　　The initials were grand,
　　Call them "City Dump" band
As their C. D. 3 tee shirts proclaimed!
*The Ithaca College Percussion Ensemble, on tour,
played at this 4th-6th grade school in Poughkeepsie,
N.Y. Their band director, Ray Lowery was our
keyboard ensemble jazz arranger.*


Fire and Smoke


Maybe thousands of years, if you please,
Is the age of the tom-tom, Chinese,
　　With its red and gold shell
　　And a dragon as well
Whom your playing had better appease!

On a Roll: Holland

I've seen bandsmen riding on camels
And other large four-legged mammals,
  But my latest band treat
  Was a bicycle fleet!
Yes! With drums, all in sunny enamels!


1920's Cuba, the Law

We the culprit have found, accuse it!
Let nobody make it or use it!!
  With this conga drum banned
  All over the land
Unrest will calm. Revolt? Defuse it!


Dr. Yes!
Sooth the Savage Breast

Far north to farthest south location
Echoes the shaman's invocation
  With drum, beads and rattle,
  Joined in benign battle
To make the ill well is his validation.

It's Ben, Again*

When you're booked to play a concert in Salonica,
And you have a part that calls for glass harmonica,
    Remember: rub it, you don't blow it;
    It's not that "mouth harp" as we know it,
But more like doing dishes in the sink, exotica.

It began to fade away after while,
Though not because its sounds had lost their style,
    But its players in service
    Suffered maladies nervous
Very serious, impervious, and vile.

So they retired it to museums various,*
Now, its existence, unplayed, is quite precarious.
    Though decay they may flout
    It's still Franklins's great clout
That allows us their pleasure, just vicarious.
*There is one in the Boston Museum of Fine Arts
Musical Instrument Collection, and a man in the area
is now (since this was written) making new versions of
it— avoiding the stress provoking elements, I hope.

A Dram O'Drum

It'd keep a dead piper in motion,
Would this drum laddie's excellent potion.
    And no sane man would knock it,
    This fine Glen Drumnadrochit,
A dark single-malt aged Scotch notion.

That you'll find it in fiction, I'm sure,*
But dispensers of lotions that cure
    May not give a divot,
    Except for Glenlivet,
You'll just have to search, lads. Endure!
*"The Burglar in the Library"
Lawrence Block, A Dutton Book, 1997.


Stamping Tubes

Thicker bamboos tamping Bonks and Binks
While thinner ones make more like Tonks and Tinks
    With different lengths
    For sounding strengths,
You'll tamp and stamp a vampy groove, methinks.

for Guillermo and Zulema
## Pampas

On the great Argentinian "plano,"
Can a very dramatic soprano*
    Have a soaring discussion
    With fifty-three percussion,
Or coo to Alberto, "piano?"

*"Cantata para América mágica (1961)"
by Alberto Ginestera (1916-1983)
We were together in Buenos Aires, 1970, when
he met me at the airport and drove me to my
hotel. Next day he left for Switzerland, and the
European premiere of his opera, "Bomarzo", not
to return, since the military government would not
allow performances of much of his music.


## That! Whistle

The whistle we need is not "the Bacall,"
"If you need me, just whistle," kind, at all—
    Though it has its own place.
    Ours, with nobody's face,
Is a train's, birds, a cop's or . . .
Well, maybe it is a "Bacall " after all!

Don't Howl! Roll!

Way back in B.C., in 2000, we heard
The kettledrums thunder as some man would gird
    Up his loins, then he'd pound
    Out a great roaring sound
Each time the Mesopotamian full moon occurred.


Poetic Materialism?

Omar Khayyam, would he really speak so:
"Ah, take the Cash, and let the promise go,
    Nor heed the rumble
    Of the distant drum."*
Bread, jug and dame? The same Omar we know?
* No. 13, 3rd Edition


El Viejo

Hey man! Dig Señor Tito Puente!
¡Quel hombre! He's still swinging plenty!
    His timbales front the band—
    Where else, this senior firebrand?
Admired by all the younger cognoscenti!

## Tin, Yet

It isn't just a bit of prattle,
Talk of drummer's playing rattle.
    Elliott Carter
    Doesn't barter:
Pocahontas? She won't tattle.


## Field Trips

Serge Prokofiev: maraca?
Is there a guiro in Le Sacre?
    Who'd have guessed?
    We all are blessed!
Let's not prejudge, but just "attacca."


## Tribal Court

The drums and gongs of an African court
Accompany the judge's sentence report.
    There will be no more rant,
    Of the plaintiff's harsh chant,
Just the judge and the drums and the gong's retort.

Lucky Pierre's Wife

The strangest drum that I ever saw
Was French: "The Cry of the Mother-in-Law."
    "L'Cri de la belle mére"
    Is a friction drum rare,
And it sure rubs Pierre's <u>wife</u> the wrong way!


"Tête de Bois"

"To write this concerto I'll use my head,
    Not do something foolish," Jacques Perrot said.
        So he whacked with a mallet
        On his cranial palette,
Wrote it down, doused the light, went to bed.


Little Boys and House Guests

When dinner time came I loved goulash,
In orchestras it was the czardas;
        But when company'd say,
        "Dear boy, you <u>must</u> play!"
I'd <u>announce</u>! and play! "<u>Hell</u> on the Wabash!"

Alcione
An opera by Marin Marais
Prod. Paris, Feb. 18, 1706


In attempting a musical storm
He would need a snare drum to perform:
    Storms with snares rather new
    In an orchestral brew,
Let alone within opera's norm.

So let's hear it for Marin Marais,
A rousingly hip "Hip Hooray!"
    He wrote great stuff for gamba
    (Had he known, maybe samba!)
And "to play up a storm" paved the way.


for Brian Duguid
Weeds


A Scotch weaver who loved to play kettles
Got his timpani mixed with his hettles:
    In the music he'd read
    He would find Harris Tweed
And his mallets were all full of nettles.

Bones

On the banks of the Thames (not the Rhone's)
Lived a drummer of sorts, name of Jones.
    Only bar-b-qued ribs
    Were the fare of his nibs,
Not from pigs, but the large ones from roans.

The real reason his came from a horse
Was the taste, though they were a bit coarse.
    Then each night in the band
    When he played them by hand,
"Mr. Bones" was his nickname, of course.

His sweet neighbor, a lovely old crone,
Often offered him tea and a scone.
    But he shunned other foods
    The way preachers shun nudes
And stayed with his miserable bones. . .

He was known as a very good worker:
No quitter, no cheater, no shirker,
    But since "Bones" had no wife,
    It was his private life
Which when questioned, made him seem a smirker.

Despite doubters, "Bones" Jones really shown,
And at dances came into his own
    Where, with bones brightly clacking,
    There were no ladies lacking,
But of afterwards, little was known.

Late at night his house echoed with moans,
An occasional shriek and great groans,
    High-pitched screaming and cries
    Plus some ladylike sighs,
And the clickety-clacking of bones
And the clickety-clacking of bones
And the clickety-clacking of bones
And the clickety-clacking . . . . . . .
And the clickety . . . . . . . . . . . . .

Sabots

Bizet's "Farandole" calls for a tabor
In his "Suite L'arlesienne," my good neighbor,
Not a drum one would play
For a fashion show, say,
But for more of a countrified labor.

Yet, the tabor in use was so varied
That to follow its path one is carried
From the cities to farms,
To some sweet maiden's arms,
Whom, if willing, might well get you married!*
*or rich!?


Poet or Peasant

A forward young fellow from Port of Spain
Tried courting a girl on an aeroplane.
He played songs on his "pan"
As the takeoff began . . .
Things didn't pan out. He'll try next on a train.

for David Borden
Dire Straits

No Odysseus, this lad from Port Byron
(A fireman in love with a siren).
    "My most favorite!" he says,
    "Give me good old Varèse,
Since I'm 'Ionization' desirin'."


The Recycling Question

If you have a big dead tree way out in back,
Don't, please, cut it down, but try this tack:
    "Would the place just really hum
    If I carved a tree-slit-drum
Like the Oceanans do?" It's worth a crack!


Little Things Mean a Lot

Is the Toy Symphony yours, Leo?, Michael?
That's Mozart, or Haydn, perhaps on their cycle,
    Avoiding acclaim
    For toy drums, the fame
That toy triangles bring and toy drummers on
                          trikes'll.

A Much Warmer Climate

You'd never go to Chichicastenango
If what you wanted was to do the wanton tango.
    You'd go to Buenos Aires
    Where the tango is the berries,
Even better than Huapangos in Durango!

Tango drummers use their set with muffled snares,
Most melodically, with ornamental flares
    Whose muffled accents lift
    The impassioned music's gift
Of tangled legs for every dancing pair.


Garçon

In a bistro abreast of the Somme
Un garçon often played his tom tóm.
    If the patrons he'd please,
    They would give him a cheese,
Otherwise, "Non encore! Nom de Nom!"

Salisbury Stake

A handsome young drummer from Sarum*
Was tempted to shout, "Ave verum
    Corpus," on learning
    His keep he'd be earning
On tambourine, in a Shah's harem!
*the older name for Salisbury.


Ms.

This percussionist played with Frank Zappa,
She was not just your casual flappa,
    But unending potential,
    And the rest, existential—
"Ruth Is Sleeping," she's taking a nappa.


Critic at Large

When Marcel Marceau plays the chimes
To hear him I've braved many climes—
    Some by air, some by boat,
    But I've not heard one note!
I'm beginning to think that he mimes.

Chef d'Percussion*

As Russell came into his prime
He availed himself of a gold chime.
   His taste soon shone through
   For it rang long and true,
Since he'd sprinkled it, lightly, with thyme.
*Russell Hartenberger, Nexus


Speed Zone*

Like marriage, like Tarzan and Simba
Or xylophone-Becker-marimba,
   It's better than not,
   When Bob B. gets hot,
That someone yell, loud and clear, TIMBA!
*Bob Becker, Nexus


West Highland*

A tom-tom performer named Cahn
Was of <u>one</u> mind while "getting it on,"
   And, again, quite another,
   When playing for mother,
Where he seemed rather "hey nonny non!"
*Bill Cahn, Nexus

Ding Dong Daddy*

There's a fellow, named Wyre, so legend tells,
Who travelled the world from the darkest cells
    To the sunniest plains
    Searching rocks, searching canes
To find very particular bells.

He found giant ones, great heavy "bongs,"
Little "angel bells" for baby's songs
    Made of silver and brass,
    Some festooned, some like glass,
Which you play with most delicate tongs.

And even the tiny young tots
Can play on his earthen red pots,
    Since bells— terra cotta,
    Are what he's gotta lotta,
From "itsy-bitsy" to big as yots!
*John Wyre, Nexus

41

Dynamic Personality*

Now Robin, Toronto, musician,
Being married, receiving permission,
     Could play flute and drum
     For a sizable sum
To bring about boredom's attrition.

What's more, and its worthy of mention,
He could further command your attention
     By playing so loud
     That he'd gather a crowd,
Be arrested and land in detention.
*Engelman, Nexus


The Anvil Chorus

Music for anvil seems oxymoronic,
Yet opera's smithies might find in it tonic.
     So, I think, pound for pound,
     That their use is still sound;
"Heavy metal", for sure, "supersonic!"

"Pop-you-lair-it-tee"

You know, if its 'country,' surely its washboard
That's scratching FM in your runabout's dashboard.
   They strum it with thimbles
   They've purchased at Gimbels
With Big Apple dough from their country band's
                                cash hoard.


Bam!! Boo!!

Tropical folks make a boobam drum.
Large and small sizes arow they may come,
   Like a kind of a keyboard
   With plenty of freeboard
To move and to strike, too, like Boo! Bam!!, some.


Rock of Ages

If the sound of the stone castanet's
What you need for that dancing brunette
   Whose amplified beauty
   Distracts from your duty,
Best try Prayer Stones, the nearest subset.

Learning to Read


For percussion, the parts may be weird,
Since the number of staves may be tiered
    As in "L'Histoire du Soldat"
    Or that one liner foxtrot
Sort of "line deprived" stave we once jeered.

Sometimes what read high might sound low,
To composers a blow was a blow.
    But now they're more hip
    And they give us a tip
For the registral sound. Say "BRAVO!"

Yet, sometimes the going gets rough,
As the clefs fly and call for new stuff
    With too many to play,
    Tempos flying away
And humankind's hands aren't enough.

Then producers slide up and say, "Heh,
Can you make this here sound?" and they neigh
    Some pained noise they think great,
    So we nod and placate
Them for now; stuff we'll later mislay. . .

And The Sixties notation's still there,
Both severe, and so free who could care.
　　　But we handle each gig
　　　Like the Man in Leipzig
Or Cambodian priests deep in prayer.

Or we're given "ad libitum" parts,
Not a scratch tells of ends or of starts.
　　　This is when our "good ear"
　　　May impress the cashier
And our $um be much more than our part's.

Yes, its always a matter of care:
Do the job with professional flair,
　　　Whether drum set or switch,
　　　It does not matter which,
Make it work! That is why we're all there.

But really, be honest now, Bunny,
Do we do it, I mean, for the money?
　　　There's that issue of PRIDE
　　　That we can't put aside,
　　　　　Still . . . yet,
What makes mama hula, Beulah, is the moolah!
Now ain't <u>that</u> the truth, really, Honey?

for my friend and colleague
Joseph Schwantner
Glasses


A conductor won't make any passes
At girls who play real crystal glasses.
    His gaze will not linger
    When they spit on their finger;
Aye, there's the rub, ladies and lasses!


AHA!


Idi and Ada and Asa, these few,
With Ara and Ava and Eve and U Nu
    Have "palindrome" names
    Like one of those games
Where backwards is forward, like Udu.

But, the Udu's a round, red clay pot;
My friends say a drum it is not,
    But when someone plays
    It very soon displays
Such "voice" that their nays are forgot.

Let it Ride!

It's the wheel we all know from Roulette,
And that drummer is playing it yette
    In Satie's work, "Parade,"
    Losing money he's made,
And the rest must be something he ette!


Victorian*

Everybody loves to hear a lion's roar,
But we hardly get to hear one anymore.
    Since the Christmases are past
    When boys gave string drums a blast,
Now, its tiny "rum tums" tumming at your door.
*In the late 19th C., lion's roar— string drums,
homemade, were played in the streets..


The Poznan Percussion Ensemble

Jerzy Zgodzinsky in Poznan did play
(My ancestor's town when in Prussia it lay),
    Sent a poster in Polish—
    My name there felt "soulish."
More than thirty years later it's still on display.

Boy Blue

The little toy drum is now rusted,
Its snares are all gone, the heads busted,
    And little Boy Blue
    Looks exactly like you,
So you know he is not to be trusted.


Bam/Bong?

Our young drummer played forte; and wrong
On the tam tam, it should have been gong.
    If the latter is tuned,
    Untold, he's marooned,
But he won't be alone out there long!


To Gordon Fung*

Looking like a layer of pagoda,
Not sounding like the Turkish one iota,
    The Chinese cymbal speaking
    To a very special peaking
From its lowest hums to sizzling ginger soda!
*Ithaca College graduate who, in 1978, put me in
touch with composers in China.

College Rings

Are there bells more alarming than storm bells?
Well, there are. Take for instance those warm belles
    Who, when out on a date
    See a ring as their fate,
Till you're saved by the clang of the dorm bells!


Crotales

As crafty a craftsman as he,
William Kraft, way out west, by the sea,
    Spins his great metal spaces
    Bowing brass in those places
That the jet stream can carry to me.


Berlioz: Tristia

"The percussion are ready, I see."
Thought the maestro, "How loud will it be?
    . . . that long army rifle—
    (A menacing eyeful—)
And why is it aiming at me?"

Dedicated to my students at Ithaca College
and to Nexus

## The Percussion Kit

Herewith you'll find a treasure chest
Resembling most a magpie's nest
(A hint there'll never be enough)
Of shiny, noisy, trashy stuff.
Composers, drummers, breeds apart,
Have used it all, its true. Let's start
With oil drums, brake drums, coffee cans,
Iron rods, tire chains, pots, lids, pans,
Plastic bottles large and small,
Fat ones, thin ones, short ones, tall,
With (inside) rattling stones or sand,
Dry seeds sizzling, peas and rice. And—
Clock chimes, ship's bells, pipes laid down,
Some suspended all around,
Rough chimes of wood or shell or glass,
And Samson's "jawbone of an ass". . .

Add whistles, whips, a pistol shot,
Sheets of tin, clay flower pots,
Spoons, wood barrels, cowbells, nails,
"Break a bottle in a pail,"
"Click your sticks," "clap, stamp and hum,"
"Spin a coin upon your drum,"

Sound car springs, pop guns, taxi horns,
Sirens, rustling papers torn!
Such riches drummers may enjoy
From cat's "meow" to kitty's toy
By which the old becomes the new—
The product of a point of view.

Thus, conservation can seduce:
"Reuse, Recycle and Reduce."

To Begin With-

The tympanum's found in urn-mosses
The space above church doors with crosses,
    The Romans raised water
    With theirs, and my daughter
Felt drops in her ear's, some.
    There's even a drum;
But let's stop now, containing our losses.

for Robin Engelman, 2/20/96
## Night Owl

A quiet young fellow with whom
A monster bass drum shared the room,
    In the dead of the night
    Would awake, flick the light,
Take his mallet and whack it KABOOM!!!
*\* Nexus 25th Anniversary Concerts*
*First Unitarian Church with WB playing his conga,*
*and Kilbourn Hall, Rochester, N.Y., Nexus.*


## Iron Deficiency?

If you find yourself needing some refills
After Verdi's great chorus for anvils,
    Try "Das Rheingold" for wild,*
    "Le Maçon," Auber's child,
Then Varèse you can play to a standstill.
*\*18 of 'em!*


## One of Us?

You'll find London press praise, if you look,
Though you'll have to select the right book.
    Glass harmonica master,*
    None better (or faster)
Than Christoph Willibald Gluck.
*\*1746, two concerts in London*

World Music Strikes Home

His wife having found India's jaltarang;
Filled small bowls with water until they sang.
    He came home at six
    For his meal, she said, "Fix!"
So he boiled midst her, "pling, plung, plang,"
    Wooden spoons tapping, "plung, pling,
    plang, plung, pling, plang, ploong,
    ploing, pling, plong, pleoung
    plang, plung, pling, plang
    plewng, plong, plung
    pluing, plong,
    pleennngg
    plinginginginging

for Yasinore Yamaguchi
NOH DICE!

An O-Daiko from friends in Japan
Didn't fit into my drumming plan,
    But when I said, "No,"
    They just countered with, "Go!"
And I lost my whole set, mama san!

53

Symphony 100 "The Military"


Papa Haydn soon took to the switch,
Not for discipline, but for the pitch,
    Which made more like a buzz
    While the real beater was
Much more firm, so the band wouldn't twitch.


Conch


When I hold the conch shell to my ear
I hear oceans from some ancient year
    When the beach held no trash—
    Just the pure water's splash,
And an earlier man seems so near.

When I hold plastic jugs to my ear
What I get is pollution and fear,
    That if things get much worse
    Then "beach" will mean "curse"
And there'll be nobody there, or here.

Mulebells— High Notes: 1829


On Spain's mountain trails sharply curving,
Our Ambassador, Washington Irving,
    With the muleteer's rough song
    And the mulebells "dang dawng"
Found both height and the bells most unnerving!


Cro-Nexus


Drag your lithophones from stage to stage,
That was the job in the old Stone Age.
    And you had no choice
    When cro-fans gave voice,
Since heavy rock bands were all the rage!


"Variations for 4 Drums and Viola" (1959)


Take yourself with violist, Phi Beta,
And 4 drums, then, into the "theatah"
    With Michael Colgrass's tune;*
    Polished bright as the moon
Shining clearly from Auckland to Etah.
*We remember the "original" Period record jacket!

John Lee

A young drummer came into a garden store
Hit a flower pot, listened, then more than a
score!
     In tune with the flowers
     He did this for hours,
Bought the tiniest three and they showed him
the door.

*"The Drums of Summer" (9 graduated tiny clay drums)
for the Austrian World premiere on July 12, 1997.
Meadows Wind Ensemble, Jack Delaney, Director.


Flat Out

The Bell Plate is not for a meal,
Though for some folks it does have appeal.
     To play a fine trill
     Takes a wee bit of skill
In bringing its beater to heel.


It's the Pits

Treating "Folies Berger Drummer's Itch,"
Doc prescribes, when one's starting to twitch,
     That you eat only scallops,
     Play only the galops,
'Cause Doc says that they're really a stitch!

56

## Knocking

No female may visit or dwell
Where the monks of Mt. Athos live well:[1]
    Fish and olives abound,
    And a Soundboard to pound[2]
Calling brothers to prayer from their cell.

[1] *the holy mountain, Khalkidiki Peninsula, Greece,*
*Eastern Orthodox monasteries from the 6th century.*
[2] *a thick wooden board, from the Greek, Sémantron.*

## Gig

I answered an ad for a drummer
To play in a band for the summer:
    Two saxes, guitar
    And an ape on sitar—
Couldn't swing on a rope! A Bummer.

## ORG

"Logging on" needs no computer, friends.
Just hollow out a log, closed at both ends,
    Make a mallet of some length,
    Whack the log with goodly strength,
And we'll hear the, "BONK DOT COMing as you send.

for Jim
The Saga of Nellie

A dancer named Nellie, quite nervous,
Tried to put all her shakes at the service
    Of her cute pelvic girdle,
    An idea quite fertile
Till things ground to a halt on the surface.

Along came a letter, young Trimble's,
Including two small finger cymbals:
    Nellie, not one to linger,
    Put one on each finger
As he'd written, then danced! O so nimble!

Soon she'd danced her way into his life
And, as hoped, she became his dear wife;
    And now in the night
    From their house without light
There are echoes of cymbals most rife. . .

Oh, a subtle campaign she did wage,
For she longed long and hard for the stage,
    So young Trimble then booked her.
    She hit! Agents hooked her
As "Nelly the Belly," the rage!

There were others, she soon ground them down,
And the best fled when she came to town;
    Till one day from afar
    Came a brighter young star,
Thus dimming the shine on our Nellie's crown.

So dear old man Trimble then eased his wife home
And built her a sweet little gilt "Bellydrome,"
    So that now, in the night
    Through the soft starry light,
Ring sweet cymbal echoes clear northward to Nome.

Church Bells
("Frost at Midnight" 1772-1834)


"... the poor man's only music," he says,
Unlike today's "Pops" or Joan Baez—
     Both post poet Coleridge,
     Which he couldn't controleridge.
Not a hum? Or a toot? Or a tune by Zez?*
*Confrey, Edward E., "Zez"; born 1895, composer
of Kitten on the Keys, Stumblin,
Dizzy Fingers and concert works.


Akwesane Social*


As the Longhouse fills up with the dancer's hum,
Ancient throbbings are heard from the water drum,
     And the rattles of cowhorn
     Clatter rhythms well worn
And as pure as this Mohawk continuum.
*National Geographic
Vol. 72, No. 3, Sept. 1997
(W. B. in the Iroquois Nation.)

## A Joyful Noise

Though the sistrum is played by a priest
Of the Coptic faith in the Near East,
    Did King David have qualms
    With a Copt in his Psalms?
'Cause he had one, we think, well, at least. . . .

## Knit Not

Nifty Cymbal noises need a knitting needle.
Take two, they're small, if you can butter up and wheedle
    Such a prize from your dear mother
    Sister, auntie, gram or other.
Solve your puzzle, ease your scrape, this wheedle deed'll.

## Then Blow Ye Winds

My wind chimes were made for outside;
One quarter century's winds have tried
    To blow them all down,
    But I've only found
Them down once, my dear Ruth. They abide.

Stormy Weather

There once was a thunder sheet made of tin,
The longest and widest, with wood ends, and thin.
    Oh, they'd hang it and shake it
    For Heaven's own sake, till it
Dimmed all the lights and called forth a Huge Djin!


. . . from little pipes and tabors . . .


There's Lou's Concerto for Flute and we,*
Less than "the other" by almost three,
    And simpler, maybe,
    But, watch it! Baby,
What seems so simple may humble thee.
*Lou Harrison, again.


The Unkindest Cut

Among the various traps that you own
Your scissors, perhaps, are not the best known.
    Ibert thought them handy;
    But some, not so dandy.
So you may bear Ibert, quite bearishly, alone.

remembering Earle
Yoric

As the poet tropes in pearly rows
May all those artful permissive blows
    Rain kindly round their guest
    And all be thereby blessed;
Their strength the freedom that each knows.
*Earle Birney, late great Canadian poet,
with Nexus and Benson in concert, Burton Auditorium,
York University, Toronto, March 31, 1973.


for Karel
1954-61, Ithaca, N.Y.

It's not quite as simple as this,
Though there's hardly a concert he'd miss
    When he was in town
    And we laid it down;
Friend Husa and we, *sui generis*.

Brag Sheet

After young Benson played timpani,
And before he would seemingly primpani,
    He would pound the snare drum
    While he'd sing, dance and hum,
On the cheap, and all night, and not skimpani.


Whistler

Some whistles are soft like a night train wail
Looking for someone, lonely and frail.
    Some are strident and crude,
    Animistic, some rude,
But we play them all: rail, quail, nightingale.


Brass, But Not Brass

The tubaphone requires no coin deposit.
It's name allows confusion, I would posit.
    No bass telephone to peal,
    But a tubal glockenspiel;
When you've finished you can put it in your closet.
*Aram Katchaturian needs one.*

The "Zero?" Drum

"Tacet" doesn't mean that you can "take it!"
And improvise a storm and really "make it!"
No, it's quite another facet
Of our art is Latin's "Tacet:"
"Make silence" until noted; please don't break it.


That Puget Sound!*
1997


In the San Juan Islands Orca Parade
Those lady marimbists, Oh, how they played!
On their flatbed truck wailing
We looked up to them, hailing!!
For the high-keyed music those maidens made!!!
*Orcas Island, Fourth of July


Sugar


Cuban conga man, sugar supreme,
With Dizzy's new, great, big band dream.
Chano Pozo, his name,
Made latin bop's game,
Had a huge hand in this cream of the cream!

Counting

The most hair raising/hair losing tests
Are orchestral works filled with long rests.
    When you can't hear a clue
    'Cause you're nervous and new
And a counterpoint pounds in your breast.

It's the nights when you're trying to sleep,
But you're counting out rests and not sheep
    So you won't miss the boat!
    God forbid! Be the goat!
When your cymbal crash tops off that sweep!

There are meters that constantly change.
(My hair looks like I have the mange!)
    First it's 2, then in 3,
    Then in half that, then free!
How I wish I was home on the range.

Where the beer and the cantelope lay,
That's the kind of stuff I like, for pay!
    You come in when it rains,
    That's what's called for in brains,
But there's not been a phone call all day. . .

So, I'll just have to count right, I guess.
Well, I don't mean, "I guess," I mean, Yes!
   'Cause it ain't any easier,
    It can only feel queasier
If I don't, and my Doc says, "No Stress!"

One-two-three, four and five, six and seven
Eight-nine-ten, and another's eleven,
    Plus five is sixteen.
    So sweet and so clean!
Look, I'm counting I'm counting. It's Heaven!

In the section, I'm shining of late,
Not playing, but all of the hair's left my pate.
    But if Head's Up is In?
    Then, I'm <u>In</u>! In with Skin!
And I'm counting on you, my stand-mate!
I'm counting! I'm counting! I'm counting! I'm counting!
I'm counting! I'm counting! I'm counting! I'm counting!
I'm counting! I'm counting! I'm counting! I'm counting!
I'm counting! I'm counting! I'm counting! I'm counting!
I'm counting! I'm counting! I'm counting! I'm counting!

Laugh, Clown

"I'm getting so sick of just "BOOM!,"
Pagliacci moaned, in his dressing room.
 "With lessons each day
  I can double! More Pay!
I Pagliacci, Toot! Ching-Ruff!, Wheet! BOOM!"


for Sarah*
The Grail and the Frail

There's still that old drummer from far off Metz
Always seeking the perfect stone castanets.
 In each wood, beach or town,
  Every time he looks down
There's one better! And the better it gets.

His discards piled up as high as his house
Have frightened his dog and displaced his spouse,
 Who now roams the Sahara
  In a diamond tiara
Writing notes in the sand to that louse!
*7/4/97, Dallas, rehearsals of "The Drums of Summer."
"Sarah" played flute and stone castanets she'd selected,
"replaced" by her library boss who found "better stones."

68

Brain Food?

Some fish are drummed up from the deep
Some are "grunts," some are "groupers"
                              you keep
    And some are called "drum,"
    Who must be so dumb
That they can't tell real drumming from
                              "bleep!"


Newpan

Carribeans may play on their pan
And Balkans, too, on their tupan, can;
    Both like drums, not the same.
    It's a wonderful game
Is our finding new sounds, I'm a fan!


Don't Be Lulled!

Maestro's Lully's baton was taller than he,
Through the orchestra's roar stamping One!
                        Two! And Three!

    Till he stamped his big toe
    A huge Ooo! Oh! Ow! Blow!
A smaller baton's, perhaps, better for thee.

(His passion for tempo, soon after this date,
  And because of it, ceased, for Lully, the late.)

Percussion Handiwork

So gentle a man, Mr. Berio,
Who can snap his finger so gently, so—
    See "Sequenza III"
    Where its at and you'll see—
Oh! so genteel the handiwork, as you all know.

And then if you look in "Passagio"
Of the selfsame Luciano Berio,
    Why, Laud, Laud, Laud,
    In there, he says, "applaude,"
Which just <u>proves</u> that you never can tell, you know.


Oral Percussion

The haughty clicked their tongues in disdain.
Karlheinz Stockhausen does this, too, in the main,
    In a very varied range
    For a tiny timbral change;
Such a tart and tasty segment is our gain.

Not Portable

I'm thinking of using that iron mine,
That Hibbing Bowl. Its not a pit, I'd opine!
    My, how it would resonate
    With the right tools to detonate!
I'm waiting for PAS to give me a sign.

With an eye out for special effects,
I'd crash cars there, the Oedipus Wrecks,
    Tunnel down near the edge,
    Then climb in with my sledge
And give 'er a haul heard clear down to Tex!

A formidable force at its peak,
As a bowl drum, its surely unique!
    So much of a groove
    That the town had to move*
Two miles South! This is not for the meek!

*Because of the open-pit mine expansion in 1919, Hibbing,
Minnesota, was moved two miles south. Now, given my
drum concept and with some radio contact we might have an
ensemble made of Maine silo bongos, the Hibbing Bowl drum,
and some grain elevator-boo-bams I've had my eye on in
Kansas. The Lava tubes in Hawaii would pretty well give us
national coverage. Though restricted in place, it would
have to be considered "an ensemble at large."

Zildjian
1623-1998


Onomatapoetic succession foretold
Of alchemists changing base metals to gold.
    None other the same,
     Each sound is their name:
Three hundred sssseventy-five!
                 craSHHHHing!
                     yearszzzzz-old!


for Tim
"Gene and Benny"


How often and long is the echo
Of its freshness and swing, tight and secco.
    "Sing, Sing, Sing!" was its name.
     Now new tunes play its game,
But they don't match that bit of Art-Deco!*
*perhaps "late" Art-Deco.

Those Other Drums*

When you sag and the beat limps a bit,
Or the twinkle's beginning to quit,
   Being drumbled is in
   Where your "kicks" have been,
So the doldrums, disarmingly, fit.

When Trivandrum's the end of your fling,
And your humdrum existence can't sing,
   Ask a panjandrum gray,
   "Should I call it a day,
To be left feeling drumly, old thing?"

A conundrum you'll hardly want much!
Every faced one? Been in one, as such?
   Psychologists see 'em,
   But not one per diem,
So, a hike on a drumlin may help, a touch.
*there are eight here.

The Trout Quintet?

Need a ratchet for something genteel?
Then you use a good fly-fishing reel:
    Just put it on "clicker"
    And it'll work slicker
Than spit on a fast ball, for real!


Missed by a Hair

The man who is playing the Dumbek
Stands too close to that fellow on Rebec!
    Mr. R. should watch out
    For that Dumbek guy's clout
Or his hairpiece is not worth one Kopek.


South of the Border

For rhythm the key word is "claves"
While for food, cloth and drink its "agaves"
    For soul and the rest
    Their "corrido" is best,
But Toccata-wise its Carlos Chavez.

And Then Some . . .

They named a dance after a drum.
If you ask me, I think it was dumb!
    The dance? Called the Conga,
    A line that grew longa,
'Til the parts were as great as the sum!

Living Languages

To think that the German word "glochen"
Speaks of "bells" is to some of us schochen.
    And adding on "spiel"
    Just to say that they "peal"
Is too much and mein mind is geblochen!

Remedial

Like chirping, undisciplined chicks!
Careless habit, that clicking of sticks.
    Who can't understand?
    Clicks ain't in the band!
(unless written there) Please, let us ficks!

for Gordon Stout
## Close Encounters of the Best Kind


Crawled up this two-laner with shoulder so slight
As the valley fell quickly and deep to the right,
    When, as if posing out there,
    In the high mountain air
Was a Mexican Marimba all shiny and bright.

I stepped on the brake, eased it over with care
To see what was up, there was noone out there!
    On the ground some crude sticks—
    Picked up four, played some licks,
Then hammered "Zandunga," a Zapotec air.

¡Aiee, toca la marimba, estimado señor!"
Someone called, as they climbed to see more
    Of this blonde-headed gringo
    Play like Yanqui Domingo
On the roadside to Taxco's front door. . .

Imagine a trio of resting musicians,
I'd broken "siesta," their short intermission-
    As they awaited their ride
    With "itself" strapped topside
To our fortunate next juxtaposition:

For Conjunto Marimba Maria would play
In the club at the place we were hoping to stay.
    Then we all had siesta,
    Saw the Silver Fiesta,
And the trio and I played the long night away!
*a true story, Christmastime, 1961, enroute Acapulco-Taxco
by car, with my wife and three little kids.

Reciprocity, 1957*

When the music has ended, you clap.
If its Benson's, beware of that chap,
    Since he might clap right back
    With the encore attack
Of a handmade octet in your lap.
*"Variations on a Handmade Theme," written for
the eight members of the Ithaca College Percussion
Ensemble as an encore, avoiding repetition from the
program or new setups— one minute, memorized,
player at stage-front, after bow.

Warm-up Symbol

When I want my hi-hat to "shick" quick
I depend on my left-handed stick trick.
    It's a "nick" flick entreaty,
    Like the globetrotters "Sweetie",
That gets me agroove in a "Boomchik!"
*11/6/96
*Regents Palace Hotel*
*Buenos Aires*


"The King of the Drums"

I first saw "Chick" Webb when aged ten.
Ella Fitzgerald was with him when
    The "King," high on his seat,
    Blurring— fast in "White Heat,"
Was my image exotic! Still is, now as then.


Hippocratic Percussion

Somewhere every second a medic
Is thumping a back for sounds Vedic;
    This orbital consonance
    Of timpanic resonance
An organic ensemble aesthetic.

The Craftsman Crosscut Cremona

Swooping note to note like a bad soprano,
Vibrating like he's had too much Cinzano,
    He bows away on what appears
    Fifteen bucks would buy at Sears.
Yet, his heart speaks through his "mano a mano."


Mickey's Place

Join in the circle and play on a drum;
Just keep it simple, and soon, crumb by crumb,
    You'll drop inhibitions,
    Relax tight positions
And feel human again, glad you've come!


Wild Thing

There once was a lion in the Serengeti
Who traded his roar for a plate of spaghetti.
    The drummer who traded
    Was ever elated,
With the roar-on-a-string in his kit at the ready!

"The Original Rochester
Afro-American Junk Band"
(1975)


Out the window Almita called, "Good!
Now, do it again," (as good teachers should!)
    And the words of their "rap"
    Had the bite and the snap
Of their life, black and white, in their 'hood.*

From the bottles and trash of their alley
Rhythms flowed through the Genesee Valley—
    Elementary school age
    Both street savvy and sage
Like a band booked by Salvatore Dali.

With Almita, I wanted to hire . . .
"Just some cookies and pop they'll require"—
    So, at Eastman, like pros—
    Oh, the temperature rose!
And the audience caught fire entire. . .

On a later date morning in May
They came to join Nexus and play:
    With no hint of shyness
    For Nexus, Your Highness,
As one, made the Eastman School sway.

Now twenties and thirties, selective,
Away, more mature and effective,
    Some musicians . . . a writer . . .
    Some broader, some brighter . . .
O, the echoes in this retrospective!
*Almita Whitis, mother of two of the boys, Christopher 10,
Jonathan 6. It was 1975 and they did their own rap
from direct experience. Chris is now a writer of plays,
prose and composes music. Jonathan's a professional
musician. Michael Clifford is also a musician. His mother,
Joyce, was involved in transport, etc. for these boys
and girls. They had a rather sensational concert life
for their age— their innocent youth and their
swinging paint cans, bottles, jugs, old car seats,
and assorted other found instruments.

## SJBO

It's rudimental knowledge, Swiss, is cheese;
And Swiss rudiments, friend drummers, if you please:
    They'll elegantly curl
    A swirl or two and hurl
A thunderbolt with flair and greatest ease.
*on tour with the Schweizer Jugend Blasorchester,
Felix Hauswirth, conductor, 1988.


## Tobermory*

When the pipers I hear in the air,
How I hasten myself to be there
    Where the drums with a snap,
    A small flourish and tap,
If I had some, 'd put curl in my hair!
*Isle of Mull, Scotch Games Day.


## Simple Gifts
## Ethiopian Picnic (New Guinea, too)

The drummers with families on a day at the beach,
Dig a tunnel, not deep and an easy reach;
    On its top bridge of sand
    They may drum with soft hand
Gentle rhythms that friends give to each.

1775-76

With "a little barrel drum" the drummer led
And "knocked . . . with little clubs" its leather
                                                    head.
    Yankee Doodle is the tune
    Seeking freedom, hoping, soon.
American Broadside*, handset, A to Zed.
*hand set printed handout used to rouse the populace.


Air for Percussion*

It looks like a big bass-drum skeleton
With a loose canvas shell-almost tarpaulin.
    A crank makes it whirl
    So its loose skirt will swirl
And shriek till your spine is pure gelatin!
*wind machine


Radio Daze *☆z

A midwestern drummer named Humphries
On a broadcast turned into a Chumphries.
    When his solo went weird
    All the audience hierd
A succession of short, wicked, Lumphries.

"The London Times: 1890"*

Being lead army drummer, and Brit.,
You'd a "cat-o-nine-tails" in your kit,
    So that, when the court ruled,
    You'd be ready and schooled
To flog the guilty one's back a bit.

To insure that the sentence was tidy and fair,
The mandate included your drum-major there
    To count all the strokes
    On those poor "bloody" blokes
So there'd be no omissions for friendship foursquare.
(Nor, perhaps, a wee bonus just to be debonair.)
* Oxford English Dictionary, "drum."


Good Behavior

Santana's band's my favorite brand,
The next best thing to just drums at hand.
    The beat's a true groove
    With "zip," too, to move
This mixed-up gringo latin gourmand.

## A to Z

This percussionist, one Michael Udow,*
Wished to dance special notes at first, somehow:
    When a crash came for cymbal,
    Both alert and quite nimble,
He'd leap, twirl, crash!, bow. (But don't ask him now.)
*Interlochen 1965-6, I remember.


## Birthday Greetings

Right-front rode the timpanist from Clyde,
In Her Majesty's Horse Guards, astride
    His black and white stallion
    Which he rode like a galleon,
While the Queen, as he passed, sat aside.*
*to review them, and, side-saddle


## Those Were the Days

The forties, the age of our rim shot,
And quieter things like the ink blot.
    The Millenium, they say,
    Makes those "ins" "out," passé:
The rim-shot the drummer's lot's not!

Semper Fi, Ret.

Understand that Andy played drums,
His photos now are worth huge sums.
    Master Gunnery Sargeant
    With chemistry argent,
The Eye of letter I and 8$^{th}$ become!

Fatten Up

The Salvation Army I've seen
Raising funds with their big tambourine,
    With my thin jingle stick
    I can't do the same trick.
Is my stick or my Credo too lean?

I Have a Beef!

Among the cowbells I slowly browse,
Some for sambas, some salsa allows.
    They all seem like clones
    By looks and by tones—
So many cowbells and so few cows.

for Tom Everett
Ivy Covered Percussion


Faxing Harvard is easy for some,
But its daunting for others who'd come
    To the band for a trial
    (Drummers deep in denial),
(Six, one, seven) four, nine, six, plus DRUM.*
*from the stationery


for Stomu Yamashita
Initial Intention


If "being a star" ever hits you,
Where will you find one that fits you?
    Heavens! I've an idea!
    Try "Cassiopeia"*
By our late great dear friend, Takemitsu.
*premiered by Stomu with the Chicago Symphony Orchestra,
Ozawa conducting, 1975. Nine years earlier, Stomu played
timpani in my ballet, Bailando, while a student at the
Interlochen Arts Academy as was Michael Udow. Mike Ranta
was their percussion teacher. I was there 1965-6 on a special
project for the Ford Foundation in which Michael Udow was
enrolled. Small World . . . and with Nexus in attendance at
Toru's premiere, returning to Toronto with Toru, and all of us
together there for a week, etc., etc., etc. Toru passed away on
February 20, 1996, as WB and Nexus were to play a 25th
Anniversary concert together.

Juan

To play real latin stuff in Ohio
Get John Beck there to play the chocallo.
    If you must play it nearer,
    Then its cheaper and clearer,
There's a great place just one block from Scio.*
*The Eastman Theatre and School of Music are
one block away, where this Past President
of the PAS has spent more than thirty years.


PP

"Ostinato Pianissimo,"
  Mr. Cowell, wouldn't you know.
    Genteel drums,
    Piano strums.
Henry's elegantissimo.


Artillery Sclerosis

For the double N cannon, Rossini,
Since the next fifteen years are linguini.
    Then comes old 1812
    Into which I won't delve.
For my Fourth of July? Dry Martini.

Remembering Chatur Lal, tabla master.
## Ragatime

The tabla and banya a fine pair are,
Especially blended in with sitar.
    Add a dash of tambura,
    A bit of bravura
And the shade of a great deodar.*
*a cedar

## Zaire*

If you wanted to frighten your adversary,
You would march to the stomp of your Janissary.*
    The jangling and stuff
    Often proved quite enough—
Had them running away into February!
*from Turkish: Yenicheri, "new troops," which implied
threat probably frightened them away. It is also called
the "Turkish Crescent" or the "Jingling Johnnie."
The great army band of Zaire used two when I saw them
in Brussels in 1985. Zaire is now called Congo.

Remembering my friend, Morris Bishop
## Cantata No. 911


The soloist screeched (the conductor's rich wife)
While all in the orchestra played for their life,
    Was never such odium
    On any podium,
Confidence fading and no lack of strife.

The maestro, confused by the flat and the sharp
And who was the culprit, the flute or the harp—
    Madame Mezzo, meanwhile,
    Carried on in her style
With her head in a posture by Twyla Tharp.

As the trumpet blared forth in the key of high B
From a part that was written for blaring in C,
    Oh, cacaphony roared,
    So much blood pressure soared
That a doctor in house raised his fee. . .

The orchestra, drenched with errata,
Then did what they thought that they oughta:
    Some quit, some resigned,
    Some went out of their mind,
As the maestro ad libbed a fermata.

Against odds, the bass drummer held out,
But our mezzo fell into a pout.
    Not the wisest decision,
    There were hoots of derision
And the evening wound up in a rout!

With Symphony Hall a real mess,
They cleaned it up, under duress,
    Finding watches, fake teeth,
    One small funeral wreath,
And the back of our mezzo's new dress. . .

This wreckage of nerves and of property
Reduced the arts budget to poverty
    Their inaugural season,
    Without rhyme or reason,
The Board had no funds for a Proper Tea!

A word to the wise was most due,
To give Madame Mezzo a clue
    About music and money
    Designed for her "Honey"
Which had prompted a patron to sue:

"Dear Madame Mezzo,
            He lacks a good ear,
And you, a lack of good judgment, my dear.
    He's no podium guy.
    Why not buy him a . . . tie,
Or a boat!! Let <u>him</u> sing! And <u>you</u> steer."

for Pat Long
Water Garden: Lilies


Did you know I play drums electronic?
It acts on my work like a tonic:
    I'm playing much younger
    Instead of high-strunger,
My ideas seem fresh, embryonic.

They may laugh when I sit down to play
My electrified drumpads one day,
    But these pads that concern me
    Seem afloat, like Giverny,
I'm a painting by Monsieur Monet!


Top This


When you're buying a child's spinning top,
Tell the clerk, "In E flat." Jaws will drop!
    If yes, then you're haven'er,
    Since England's John Tavener
Spins a "Requiem" that calls for this prop.

Drums In My Heart

They are the "Women of the Calabash;"
Dance, and playing with great "panache"
    Bamboo tubes, gourds and stones,
    Such rhythm to my bones
That I love 'em with a mad, mad pash!


The Foxhunt Meets the Park Concert

The hounds chased the flutes up a tree to a crotch,
Mixing the rest so they made a great botch
    Of the Beethoven Fifth
    At the Firth of Forth, with
The timpanist guarding his Glenlivet Scotch.


The Taiko

Several strokes invoke the god of rain:
Willow strokes (the hoe) for harvest gain,
    For many farmland Japanese
    Folk festivals still practice these,
And strike with hands whenever sowing grain.

Movement

Precision and costumes you come for,
The Rockettes have nothing on drum corps,
 While the corps' roaring brass
 Is enough to break glass,
The drum strokes are movement "d'or."*
*of gold


The Damaru

You can twirl this small drum-on-a-stick,
Making two string arms pop! From the flick
 Of the balls on their ends.
 Small? A toy for young friends.
Large? It's a Nepalese worshipping pick.


for Col. John R. Bourgeois, Ret.
Semper Flam

One left if by land, two rights if by sea
Are for hopeful Marine Band drummers to be
 The audition test lick,
 Plus one you may pick;
"Marine Bayou Triplets" they'll call them,
       you'll see.*
*if they study my "New Orleans Bayou Rudimental
Technique and Crayfish Recipe Manual," that is.

My Kind of Guy

With paleo-diddles a downright cinch
He'd whack slate cymbals and not even flinch.
    In his band bearskin suit
    He could play like a brute
And never back off, though he'd doze in a pinch.

His stalactite sticks flashing in firelight red,
Each drum with a sabre-toothed tiger skin head,
    The Cro-Magnon Café
    At the end of the day
Saw Fred Flintstone on drums, as if to them bred.


Must Hear
WPS— 21453


Ravi Shankar, Alla Rahka, and Rich,
Buddy, that is, though rather a hitch;
    In "Rich a la Rahka."
    A plug of tobacca'd
Never make <u>me</u> believe such a pitch!
*World Pacific LP,
Liberty Records

War Is Heck

Legends and baubles build bonding in groups
With colors and plumage and braiding in loops.
        To inspire what counted,
        "Silver Drumsticks" were mounted
When Napoleon's drummers inspired his troops.

In toy shops along the great Champs-Élyseés
Imperial drummer boys drum on all day,
        Little soldiers for sale
        Making glory, small scale,
Seem innocent, from far, far away.
*The New Yorker, "The Good Soldier," 11/24/97.


thanks to David Moore
A Higher Power

There once was a cordless amplified psaltery
Regaling the angels with sounds cheap and paltery.!
        Yet, despite being wooed by such flattery,
        Approaching a psaltery and battery,
They encored this tasteless electric exaltery.

97

Artistes

A marimbist who made his own mallets
And his lady, a painter, in palettes,
 When dining alone
 Were oft heard to moan
By the neighbors, "Why ALWAYS
      have shallots!"


for Don
Flicks

A silent film festival? Charming.
All the technocrat public disarming
 With its straightforward stance
 And a kick in the pants,
Then the daredevil mischief alarming!

When she's run for the triangle's phone
      (made by you),
A bass drum and cymbal crash nicely will do,
 Though a slide whistle helps
 To fill in for her yelps,
When her fall shows a petticoat bottoms-up view!

Equilateral Credit


Said the smithy, "That drummer plays my angle.
It was I who first made him a triangle!
    Now he's tinging and dinging
    While others are singing
And dares call it His Music!" A wry wrangle.


Pitch to Nonpitch, 1958
Oh, That "L'Histoire . . ." Rhythm!


To arrange <u>Danse du Diable</u> for nonpitched drums?
Robin writes Stravinsky; the answer comes.
    He approves! We rehearse-
    On a box, drums diverse,
Then record, riding high! Robin hums.
*Freshman Robin Engelman (spring 1958) asked*
*if this was possible. Now he owns a dated Stravinsky*
*autograph. Golden Crest LP #4016 "Warren Benson*
*Presents Percussion— with the Ithaca Percussion*
*Ensemble." Pitch to Nonpitch who'd believe it!*

For Helen Myers
Rise and Shine!


One can't sit to play dhantal,* and, act out—
So, no story songs. You'll find that fact out.
    You decide, then, to stand
    And your beater remand
To the trash, then you act till you're whacked out.
*iron, one meter high like a J and struck with an iron rod.
Sitting to play and self-accompaniment both died out.
The stories survive. India, Fiji, Trinidad.


For Tom Hampson
Big Noise, 1938


"Bring your bass a bit closer there, Bobby,
And whistle," said Ray, in the lobby.*
    When "Big Noise" began to play
    Ray leaned over and had his way
Making drumsticks on bass the new hobby.
*Ray Bauduc, drums, to Bobby Haggert, bass, in Bob
Crosby's "Bobcats." The tune, "Big Noise From
Winnetka," written by Haggert in 1938, was a "hit"
recording. Ray Bauduc was noted for very original
cymbal work, with Crosby 1938-1942.

for Ian, Adam and Sean
Seasonal Work


Ceremoniously charging with glee,
Drum elephants seem filled with esprit,
    Their Nagara full roaring,*
    Into villages pouring
To find bride-bound bachelors a she.
*elephantback mounted ceremonial Indian timpani.
Whole villages of bachelors ride them into villages
where prospective brides might be found..


Mi Casa Es Su Casa*


First, even out your long roll, two by two.
Then, liittle by little, if you do,
    You lead a fine school band
    With your ego well in hand,
And maybe they'll name one after you.
*The Garwood Whaley Music Center. Bishop
Ireton High School, Alexandria, Virginia. Dedicatory
concert 4/4/98. A Juilliard graduate, U.S. Army Band
for six years with other professional services,
a doctorate and twenty five years touring Europe
every spring with the Bishop Ireton Band;
just do that, and you're in!

## July 4th

The deep growl of the rope drum I know
As a gift from those days long ago,
    And the buoyant old fife
    Brings to tired legs life,
As the straight, simple tunes fairly glow.


## 27 Centuries*

This rare bronze Phoenician Chalkophon
Saw the building of the Parthenon.
    Of sistrums it is kin,
    Just two, supplies are thin.
Its sound, though, is still first echelon.
*7th or 8th Century, B.C., one of only two known
in the world. Auctioned at the European Fine Art
Foundation Fair in Basel, Switzerland, October
26-November 3, 1996 by Antiken-Kabinett, Frankfurt.
Architectural Digest, October 1996, p. 32.

Tote that Bell

A sixty-four hundred pound bell,
Middle c's made of metal as well.
    Octave higher your fief?
    Fifty-six hundred less beef.
That's why little one's toll our knell.

At a hundred pounds c3's quite slight,
But, if you desire the Great C's might,
    Then its six figures, drummers,
    Every pound of them hummers,
Four hundred thousand six hundred, right?

envoi

Let's be grateful
For portable stuff.
Enough's
Enough.

Again, Sam?

I come to a measure marked "bis;"
Can't rhyme "this," neither "ice," only "peace:"
    "To repeat this one measure,"
    A kind of a treasure
For the Frenchman, composer, Maurice.

Ambition

In a farmyard in far eastern Maine
Two tall silos were etched in my brain,
    I've been trying to obtain
    An enormous membrane
For my bongo conceit transmundane.

I had started to search far and wide
For Paul Bunyan's Great Blue Ox's hide
    And a great truck to fetch it
    With a great hoop to stretch it
And a chopper to fly me topside.

As I'll hang down in harness and flail,
Nearby lobsters will throw me their tail
    As the fresh, juicy oysters
    All emerge from their cloisters
And a clambake will shortly prevail. . .

But, since Babe is a legend so dear,
I must look somewhere else, though I fear
    That large hides for my needs
    Come from endangered breeds;
And linen, I'm sure, is too sheer.

So, its swimming pool liners I've bought;
Then, I've snugged them both down nice and taut.
    But when I hit staccati!
    I unearth Maine's potati!*
So the Sheriff my presence has sought.

My folks talked of Maine as "down east."
Well, I'm pretty far down, here, at least.
    Not, Get Down!, down, just down.
    Ain't no rhythm in this here town,
Just jail. And my bongos? Deceased.
* "you say poe-tay-toes"


Mr. Smooth


Never a drummer more cozy than Cole,
A stylist example both graceful and droll.
    With his set in the round
    He could blend any sound
And embed the band's groove in your soul.

Little Jack, Horner

An opera buff from Vancouver,
A fancy young shaker and mover,
    On a concert he'd planned
    For his very own band
Played "Manon Lescaut" on his Hoover.

An attachment he used with aplomb
And loudly did make the part hum,
    Till an asthma attack,
    Oh, alas and alack,
Made him jerk, and it sucked in his thumb!

He'd backed himself into a corner,
"I'll quit vacuums," he said, "be a horner!"
    So he pulled out his thumb
    And said, "Boy, that was dumb!"
Ate some pie, and seemed not a bit worner.


Fast Track

Borodin didn't mean to be mean,
When he wrote in 1/1 which was keen.
    As those measures fly by
    You must keep up or die!
To count trees from a train seems routine.

Riddler

Contradiction: the music, the name,
Maybe that's why he played his sly game—
    Percussion Constructions
    Eight Radio fluxions
Sound-Silence, Cage-Freedom,
                 the same?


PAS
I Remember

We danced alone in those "good old days,"
When "life was simpler." Yet, in that haze
    Of golden, distant summers:
    They-"musicians," We-"drummers."
But now, a PAS*de doux we praise.
* *Percussive Arts Society*


for Tim Reynish
United

American drummers will always stand
In the orchestra or the concert band,
    And when in the pit
    They'll sit just a bit,
But the English, I think, understand.

The Original

The "Violin Concerto," a coup,
By a man who is known as Lou,
    Calls for brake drums, tin cans,
    Mantle-clock chimes, but sans
Those pedigreed percussion true blue.

There's a contrabass laid on a chair,
Lacking bowing, as such, by a hair,
    But with drumsticks and things
    For light tapping its strings—
It's "col legno battuto" for fair.

Then add six iron rods all suspended.
You notice? The norms seem extended!
    Still, the whole structure's sound,
    He's his feet on the ground,
Mr. Harrison must be commended!


STOMP!

Let the striking and crashing commence,
Household "instruments" filling with dents,
    As with glee they all dance
    Wearing blue jeans for pants,
Sweeping folks off their seats, they're immense!

## Alexander Calder Joins the Band

I've only seen part of a photo,
Which suggests how it looks when in toto:
    Free-form bell-plates afloat,
    Watch your head! Then emote
On this Mobile that one plays "con moto."

The name came from friend Marcel Duchamp,*
Habitue of the avant-garde art camp:
    "They keep moving," he purred,
    "Call them 'mobiles,' good word!"
Then he stripped and descended a ramp.

One was made for composer Earle Brown . . .
. . . a percussion piece, moving and sound,
    It was called, "Calder Piece,"
    Our most moving release,
It's the only real action in town.

*painter, whose 1912 "Nude Descending a Staircase"
remains his most famous work.
Detail drawing from Cleveland Institute of Music photo,
with permission, thanks to Richard Weiner.

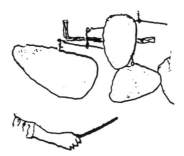

Amigo Mio
(recuerdo 1961)

A timely young fellow name Remo
Loved drumming and drums, had a
                              scheme-o,
    To make very new stuff,
    (Since there's never enough)
Nylon sticks, roto-toms, (eye agleam-o).

Like percussionists all, kept his head,
Not of hide, but of plastic, instead—
    "It won't have the sound"—
    Was the comment around,
But, in time, Remo's "head" was ahead.

Some white nylon sticks came my way
When he sent me a box for no pay—
    Free and made to my order
    For a south of the border
Percussion and research foray. . .

I gave some away for fiesta
To a band near my house one siesta
    Playing crude hand carved sticks,
    When I showed them some tricks
And we soon were compadres, the best, ah!

I gave some to real pros and to others,
To little boy drummers and their mothers;
    Now, in old Mexico,
    There's a saint named "Remo"
Who gave friendship and joy to his brothers.

Thus, though its date is belated,
It's time that this tale was related . . .
    Of, Remo, our friend,
    For his kind dividend,
¡Muchas Gracias! With interest, pro-rated!

The Critics

From buckets of bones we made clickers;
Some other new things brought on snickers,
    But we stuck to our last,
    After dark played a blast
And frightened them out of their knickers!

Every Little Bit Alps

The Almglochen's range is quite high,
Approaching high C in the sky;
    Its soft clanking beaters
    At three thousand meters
Make Swiss cheese the best thing on rye.

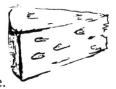

The Xmas Song

As a sideline, old Scrooge's Bob Cratchit
Was an orchestra drummer, on ratchet,
    Till he played loud and long
    During some diva's song
And she chased him all night with a hatchet!

God Hath Men

"God hath men who enter Paradise
Through their flutes and drums."
                        With prophet wise,

    Islam's Mohammed, we can see
    The One who gives to us this key:
For all our work and play and joy and prize.

Déjà vu 1950*

If one will's one to be a big drum,
All they need you to do is succumb,
    Then be peeled, scraped and tanned,
    And well rim-tucked by hand,
While dear Harvard's museum stays mum.

On a date of importance to friends
Have them beat the drum made of your ends
    In strict time with a tune
    That's in phase with the moon
At Bunker Hill, for all that portends!
*U.S. News and World Report, December 22, 1997,
p. 74, man wills his skin to Harvard, etc. .


Unisection

When females were deemed to be weaker
Career prospects could hardly seem bleaker.
    Now they win the audition,
    The males moan, "Perdition!",
And our drum sections shape up much sleeker.

We Were There


Its still the same old conflict, after all,
The human and divine, the rise and fall,
    "The wild orb of our orgies,
      Our timbrel; and thy gorges
Rang," and blended them, as we recall.
*from the Greek, Euripides (480-406 B.C.),*
*"The Bachae," lines 124-6.*
*The timbrel – a tambourine.*


That's Show Biz


He sent for two washtubs from Sears
(We wouldn't need ours yet for years),
    But no Lou Harrison,
    George Eastman's comparison
For two of his rear chandeliers.*
*\*painted gold, they hang in the rear of the Grand*
*Balcony of the 3400 seat French Renaissance*
*Eastman Theatre, 1920's. Lou Harrison calls for two,*
*suspended, in his Violin Concerto, 1950's.*

for Capt. Frank Byrne, USMB
## Putting Teeth in Your Ensemble


The jackass on the green grass gnaws
Or serves in Congress making laws,
  But when he dies
  And up he dries
Then we make music with his jaws.

Its not that "hee-haw" sound you know
But a buzzing, rattling kind down low.
  When they lose their juice
  Their teeth get loose
And they buzzz when you bump 'em, row on row.


envoi


In your Bible study class
Note "the jawbone of an ass."*
Samson had a further use:
He used jawbones for abuse.
*Judges 15:15

## Postlude

These drum lines I've kept very orderly,
Nice and clean, neither shady nor borderly,
   Never wantonly crude,
   Downright evil or rude,
Yet, not suited for Musical Quarterly.

# Acknowledgements

The admirable examples of my late friend Morris Bishop and the countless other writers of limericks whose terse tickles have teased me for tens of years, the gifts of information from friends like Robin Engelman and Bill Cahn of the incomparable Nexus ensemble, the incredible resources of lexicographer Nicholas Slonimsky, the rich literary illustrations of the great Oxford English Pictionary, and, the untold number of general references, percussion books, instrument catalogs, record jackets, articles, magazines, music scores and concerts, concerts, concerts that have informed me over more than six decades are what have fed this attempt to have some fun, note some speculations, some oddities, preserve a few interesting memories and recognize friends, colleagues and other interesting rogues.

Thank you everyone.

WB, January 19, 1999

## About the Author

*Born in 1924, and a professional performer by the age of fourteen, Benson played timpani in the Detroit Symphony Orchestra under Ormandy, Reiner, Goosens, Bernstein and others while an undergraduate at the University of Michigan where he was the percussion instructor during his freshman year, 1943.*

*After fourteen years at Ithaca College, where, in 1953, he organized the first touring percussion ensemble in the eastern United States, the second worldwide. Benson became Professor of Composition at the Eastman School of Music in Rochester, New York, from 1967-1993, where he was honored with an Alumni Citation for Excellence, the Kilbourn Professorship for distinguished teaching and was named University Mentor. In 1994 he was appointed Professor Emeritus.*

*His music is performed in over 40 countries, and more than 30 works have been commercially recorded. He has received numerous awards, including the John Simon Guggenheim Composer Fellowship, three National Endowment for the Arts composer commissions and the Diploma de Honor from the Ministry of Culture of the Republic of Argentina.*